WHEELCHAIR BASKETBALL

ETHAN OLSON

childsworld.com

Published by The Child's World®
800-599-READ • www.childsworld.com

Photography Credits
Photographs ©: John Walton/PA Wire/AP Images, cover,
1; Kiichiro Sato/AP Images, 2, 20; iStockphoto, 3 (top),
3 (bottom), 6, 11, 12, 14; Stefa Nikolic/iStockphoto, 5;
Shutterstock Images, 8; Buda Mendes/Getty Images Sport/
Getty Images, 17; Shaun Botterill/Getty Images Sport/Getty
Images, 18

ISBN Information
9781503885073 (Reinforced Library Binding)
9781503885783 (Portable Document Format)
9781503886421 (Online Multi-user eBook)
9781503887060 (Electronic Publication)

LCCN 2023937313

Printed in the United States of America

ABOUT THE AUTHOR

Ethan Olson is a sportswriter and
editor based in Minneapolis,
Minnesota. He enjoys sports, and he
has written multiple children's books.

CONTENTS

ONE MORE BASKET

Diego crossed half-court and set the basketball on his lap. The tension in the gym was growing. All of Diego's teammates were guarded. Diego hesitated. Two defenders pressed their wheelchairs against his. This made it so Diego couldn't put the ball down to dribble. He was locked in place.

Suddenly, Diego's teammate Will slipped past his defender. He was headed straight for the basket. Diego gripped the ball tightly with his right hand. He then brought the ball behind his head while using his other hand to stabilize his chair. With a swift move, Diego snuck a pass right to Will's chest. An easy **layup** put their team, the Hawks, in the lead.

The Hawks were up against their biggest rivals, the Wildcats. The game had been back and forth. And sure enough, another Wildcats bucket tied the game again at 50–50. Now the Hawks had the ball with 20 seconds left and the league championship on the line.

Wheelchair basketball gives athletes who are disabled the opportunity to showcase their athletic abilities.

As point guard, Diego took the ball up the floor. He dribbled twice, then set the ball on his lap. Now Diego could build up speed before dribbling again. He zipped by a Wildcats defender before grabbing his wheel to stop. The slick move created space for Diego to shoot.

With a quick flick of his right wrist, Diego got off a shot. He held his follow-through as the ball sailed through the air. It hit nothing but net as the buzzer sounded throughout the gym. The game was over. The Hawks had won the championship!

Wheelchair basketball is a team sport for people with different physical disabilities. Many of its rules are the same as those in traditional basketball, which is also called running basketball. The basket, court, and lines all have the same measurements. Both games consist of five players on each team. And in both, the object of the game is to score more points by shooting the ball through a basket. Most baskets are worth two points. However, any made shot outside the three-point arc earns three. A made free throw is one point. The team with the most points at the end of the game wins.

◄ **The rules of wheelchair basketball are largely the same as running basketball.**

WHEELCHAIR DIAGRAM

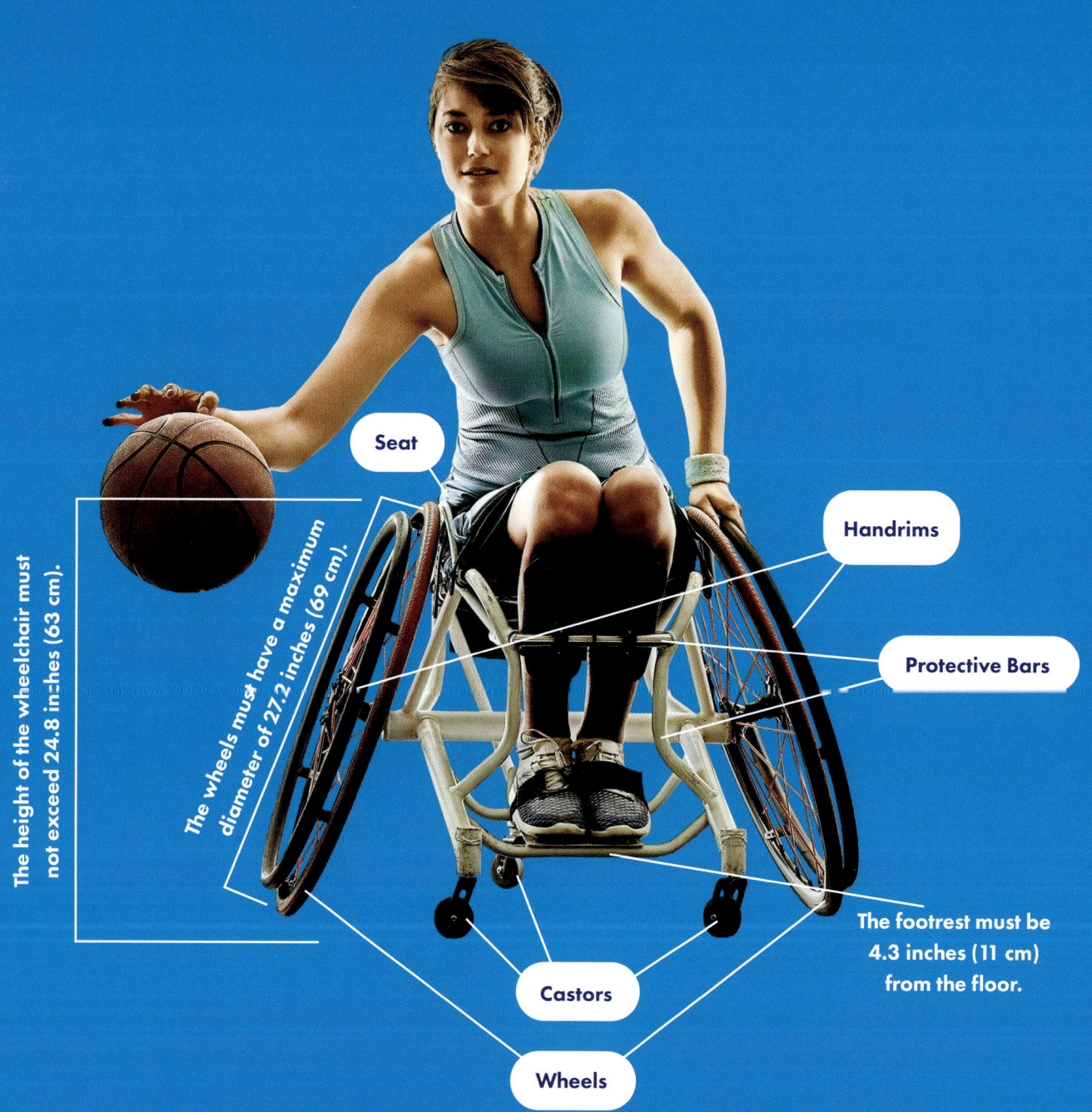

Seat

Handrims

Protective Bars

The height of the wheelchair must not exceed 24.8 inches (63 cm).

The wheels must have a maximum diameter of 27.2 inches (69 cm).

The footrest must be 4.3 inches (11 cm) from the floor.

Castors

Wheels

At its core, wheelchair basketball is very similar to running basketball. But there are key differences. One of the biggest involves dribbling. In wheelchair basketball, a player may wheel the chair and dribble at the same time. But if the ball is picked up, the player can only push their wheels twice before having to shoot, pass, or dribble again. There is no rule that forbids **double dribbling**, unlike running basketball.

There are also regulations for the wheelchairs themselves. The footrest and protective bars at the front and sides of the wheelchair must be 4.3 inches (11 cm) from the ground. Wheelchairs each have two large wheels on the back. They also have one or two smaller front wheels, called castors. Players have the option to add an anti-tip castor called "the fifth wheel." No steering wheels, brakes, or gears are allowed. Players must use their skills and strength to keep up with the high-speed action.

The wheelchair is a piece of equipment that is also considered a part of the player. Wheelchairs must meet all standards required by the International Wheelchair Basketball Federation (IWBF) to be game-eligible.

CHAPTER TWO

A SPORT FOR ALL

Thousands of soldiers came home from World War II (1939–1945) with life-changing injuries. Back then, sports were primarily set up for nondisabled people. Several new **adaptive sports** invented around this time created opportunities for those with disabilities.

Special hospitals worked with the veterans who had served in the armed forces. Meanwhile, basketball was already a popular sport in the United States. So in 1946, wounded soldiers at hospitals in California and Massachusetts began playing wheelchair basketball. The sport helped with their **rehabilitation**. However, there wasn't much structure to the sport.

Dr. Timothy Nugent at the University of Illinois helped make wheelchair basketball more organized in the late 1940s. He also helped create rules and official competitions. Nugent and the University of Illinois hosted the first official wheelchair basketball tournament. From there, Illinois became the home of the sport.

Two teammates celebrate scoring a basket.

Meanwhile in England, Sir Ludwig Guttmann treated veterans with spinal cord injuries. And in 1948 he organized the first Stoke Mandeville Games. This competition included wheelchair netball, a similar sport to wheelchair basketball.

Netball became popular in other parts of Europe. However, in 1955 an American team called the Pan Am Jets was invited to the Stoke Mandeville Games. Before long, wheelchair basketball had overtaken netball. This led to wheelchair basketball being included in the first Paralympic Games, which took place in 1960 in Rome, Italy.

Netball is similar to basketball, but there is no backboard, no dribbling allowed, and no running with the ball, among other differences.

Like the Olympics, the Paralympics is a world-wide sporting event held every four years. Wheelchair basketball was one of the original eight Paralympic sports. However, only men could play in the 1960 Games. Women's wheelchair basketball was introduced eight years later in Tel Aviv, Israel.

The Paralympics remain the sport's biggest stage. However, there are other important competitions. The first World Championships for men took place in 1975. And for women they were held for the first time in 1990. The World Championships take place every four years, like the Paralympics.

Wheelchair basketball is one of the rare Para sports with a large following outside of international play. The National Wheelchair Basketball Association (NWBA) began in 1948. As of the 2022–23 season, that organization represented 225 teams across the United States, Canada, and Puerto Rico. There were junior divisions and adult levels, as well as a Women's Division. Athletes ranged from five to 65 years old.

MAKING THE GAME

Dr. Timothy Nugent helped create the rules of wheelchair basketball. His next step was to start a league. In 1948 Nugent started the NWBA. He served as the **commissioner** for 25 years. The NWBA helped increase the sport's popularity in the United States, as well as further develop the sport's rules.

There are wheelchair basketball leagues for people of all ages.

Athletes can also compete in wheelchair basketball at the college level. The University of Illinois has the longest-running men's and women's teams. The women's team was founded in 1970. That was two years after the first Paralympic women's wheelchair basketball tournament. Eventually more women wanted to play the sport at a high level. The first game between two women's teams in the United States was held in 1973 at the University of Illinois. A few years later, in 1977, the NWBA approved a plan to create a women's division.

The NWBA developed another part of the sport called the **classification** system. Wheelchair basketball players are classified on a point system from 1 to 4.5. The lower the number, the more **restricting** the player's disability is. Each team has five players on the court at a time. Their combined rating must be 15 points or less.

CHAPTER THREE

WHEELCHAIR BASKETBALL LEGENDS

Before Steve Serio became Team USA's main ball handler, he grew up in New York. At 11 months old, Serio had surgery on his back that resulted in him being paralyzed. As an older child he grew to love the game of basketball. He played against nondisabled athletes in middle school. But his high school didn't allow him to play running basketball in a wheelchair. That's when he joined the only competitive Junior wheelchair basketball team in New York—the Long Island Lightning.

Serio was able to show off his athletic skills on the Lightning. He quickly became a talented point guard. Serio's ability to see the court and make the right passes set him apart.

Serio was in college at the University of Illinois when he made his first Paralympic appearance at the Beijing Games in 2008. His intelligence on the court helped him excel as a point guard. Team USA fell short of winning a medal in Beijing.

Steve Serio of Team USA prepares to make a move during a game against Germany at the Paralympic Games in Tokyo, Japan, in 2021. ▶

But as Serio became comfortable as a starting guard, the American men rose to the top of the sport.

Over the next three Paralympics, Serio and Team USA took home two golds and one bronze medal. Their first gold in 2016 was the first for the US men in 28 years. As a co-captain, Serio scored seven points and dished out 10 **assists** to lead the United States in the historic gold-medal game. And in the 2023 World Championships, Serio added 16 points to help his team bring home the title by one point over Great Britain.

Before the United States won gold in Rio, Canada was dominant in men's wheelchair basketball. Patrick Anderson was a major reason. He grew up in Fergus, a small town in Ontario, Canada, playing ice hockey. However, when Anderson was nine, he was hit by a drunk driver. He needed both his legs **amputated** below the knee. Anderson didn't lose his fiery passion for sports. He was able to show off his competitive spirit on the court when he began playing wheelchair basketball in 1990.

Anderson was impressive as a starter at the University of Illinois. He worked his way up to the Canadian national team in 1997. Over the next two Paralympics, he helped lead Canada to back-to-back gold medals in 2000 and 2004.

Patrick Anderson takes a shot during the gold-medal game between Canada and Australia at the 2012 Paralympic Games in London.

Team USA's Natalie Schneider shoots over China defenders during the Paralympic Games in Tokyo, Japan, in 2021.

After a silver in 2008, Canada returned to the top of the podium in 2012. Anderson was a starter during all four Paralympics.

Anderson was intense on the court. He had to be to battle under the basket for layups and rebounds. Over his first two Paralympics, Anderson averaged more than 20 points and 11 rebounds per game.

Meanwhile, Team USA ruled the women's side with Natalie Schneider on the team. Schneider began using a wheelchair in high school when a rare bone cancer was discovered in her leg. Schneider didn't find wheelchair basketball until the 2005–2006 season, after she had graduated from the University of Nebraska. She grew up playing basketball. So the movements and strategy were familiar to her.

Schneider's experience playing running basketball helped her make the wheelchair national team in 2008, the first year she tried out. She was dedicated to being a smart player and a leader. For her efforts, she was elected co-captain at the Beijing Games in China in 2008, where the United States won gold.

After winning a second gold at the Rio Games in 2016, Schneider led her team to a bronze medal at the Tokyo Games in Japan in 2021. She was the most experienced member of the women's team. Wheelchair basketball continues to grow as a sport due to incredible athletes like Schneider.

PRACTICE MAKES PERFECT

Prior to the 2021 Paralympic Games in Tokyo, China's best finish in women's wheelchair basketball was sixth place. The team began intense training in 2020. Players each had to make 400 free throws per day. This helped China win a silver medal in Tokyo. On the way, China beat the defending champion American women twice.

GLOSSARY

adaptive sports (uh-DAP-tiv SPORTS) Adaptive sports are competitive sports designed for people with disabilities. Wheelchair basketball is one of the adaptive sports included in the Paralympic Games.

amputated (AM-pyuh-tate-ed) Amputated means that a limb was removed through surgery. Some wheelchair basketball players have had their legs amputated.

assists (uh-SISTS) Assists are passes that lead to a teammate making a basket. Steve Serio dished out 10 assists to help his team win.

classification (klas-uh-fuh-KAY-shun) Classification is a system used to group athletes with similar abilities so they can compete fairly against one another. In wheelchair basketball, each player is given a classification between 1 and 4.5.

commissioner (kuh-MISH-uh-nur) A commissioner is a person in charge of the operations of a sports league. Dr. Timothy Nugent was the commissioner of the NWBA for 25 years.

double dribbling (DUH-buhl DRIB uhl ing) Double dribbling is when a player dribbles the ball after already picking it up or uses both hands to dribble. It is acceptable to double dribble in wheelchair basketball but not running basketball.

layup (LAY-up) A layup is a shot in basketball taken from underneath the basket. A layup is worth two points.

rehabilitation (re-huh-bil-uh-TAY-shun) Rehabilitation is the process of helping somebody regain physical function. Veterans from World War II used wheelchair basketball as a rehabilitation activity.

restricting (ri-STRIKT-ing) Restricting means limiting someone's abilities. In Paralympic sports, athletes are rated on a classification system based on how restricting their disability is.

FAST FACTS

+ Wheelchair basketball was developed in the United States by Dr. Timothy Nugent in the late 1940s.

+ Wheelchair netball, a very similar sport, started in Europe in 1948 for veterans with spinal injuries.

+ Men's wheelchair basketball was one of the original eight sports in the Paralympic Games in 1960. The women's competition was added in 1968.

+ Each wheelchair basketball player is given a number ranking from 1 to 4.5 on the level of their disability. The total classification for the five players on the court must add up to 15 or less.

+ At the 2016 Paralympics, Steve Serio captained the US men to their first Paralympic gold in 28 years.

+ Canadian star Patrick Anderson helped his country to three Paralympic gold medals in 2000, 2004, and 2012.

+ Through 2021, Natalie Schneider had helped the United States win two gold medals and a bronze medal at the Paralympics.

ONE STRIDE FURTHER

+ Why is it important to have sports for people with physical disabilities?

+ How do you think the Paralympic Games have helped wheelchair basketball grow around the world?

+ If you could meet an athlete from this book, what would you ask them?

FIND OUT MORE

IN THE LIBRARY

Alexander, Lori. *A Sporting Chance: How Ludwig Guttmann Created the Paralympic Games*. Boston: Houghton Mifflin Harcourt, 2020.

Herman, Gail. *What Are the Paralympic Games?* New York: Penguin Workshop, 2020.

Ouellet, Marie-Claude. *Amazing Athletes: An All-Star Look at Canada's Paralympians*. Berkeley, CA: Owlkids Books, 2021.

ON THE WEB

Visit our website for links about wheelchair basketball:
childsworld.com/links

Note to Parents, Caregivers, Teachers, and Librarians: We routinely verify our Web links to make sure they are safe and active sites. So encourage your readers to check them out!

INDEX